TRAIN YOUR BRAIN
THINK LIKE AN ASTRONAUT

Written by Alex Woolf

illustrated by David Broadbent

CRABTREE
PUBLISHING COMPANY
WWW.CRABTREEBOOKS.COM

A note from the author and publisher
In preparation of this book, all due care has been exercised with regard to the instructions, activities, and techniques depicted. The publishers and author regret that they can accept no liability for any loss or injury sustained. Always get adult supervision and follow manufacturers' advice when using electric and battery-powered appliances.

The activities described in this book should always be done in the presence of a trusted adult. A trusted adult is a person (over 18 years old) in a child's life who makes them feel safe, comfortable, and supported. It might be a parent, teacher, family friend, care worker, or another adult.

Every effort has been made by the publishers to ensure websites are suitable for children, that they are of the highest educational value, and that they contain no inappropriate or offensive material. However, because of the nature of the Internet, it is impossible to guarantee that the contents of these sites will not be altered. We strongly advise that Internet access is supervised by a responsible adult.

Facts, figures, and dates were correct when going to press.

First published in Great Britain in 2021 by Wayland
Copyright © Hodder and Stoughton, 2021

Author: Alex Woolf
Illustrator: David Broadbent
Series editor: Melanie Palmer
Series design: David Broadbent
Editorial director: Kathy Middleton
Editor: Kathy Middleton
Proofreader: Crystal Sikkens
Production technician: Margaret Salter
Print coordinator: Katherine Berti

Library and Archives Canada Cataloguing in Publication
CIP available at Library and Archives Canada

Library of Congress Cataloging-in-Publication Data
CIP available at the Library of Congress

Crabtree Publishing Company
www.crabtreebooks.com   1-800-387-7650

Published by Crabtree Publishing Company in 2022.

All rights reserved. No part of this publication may be reproduced, stored in a retrieval system or be transmitted in any form or by any means, electronic, mechanical, photocopying, recording, or otherwise, without the prior written permission of Crabtree Publishing Company. In Canada: We acknowledge the financial support of the Government of Canada through the Canada Book Fund for our publishing activities.

Printed in the U.S.A./012022/CG20210915

Published in Canada
Crabtree Publishing
616 Welland Ave.
St. Catharines, Ontario
L2M 5V6

Published in the United States
Crabtree Publishing
347 Fifth Ave
Suite 1402-145
New York, NY 10016

CONTENTS

4 Traveling to Space
6 Be Healthy and Fit
8 Know How Things Work
10 Neil Armstrong: First on the Moon
12 Make Good Decisions
14 Improvise to Survive
16 Change Your Perspective
18 Yi So-yeon: First South Korean in Space
20 Floating Free
22 Prepare to Be Lonely
24 Communicate
26 Mae Jemison: Astronaut, Doctor, and Engineer
28 Train for a Spacewalk
30 Be Curious and Observant
32 Develop Your Piloting Skills
34 Chris Hadfield: The Singing Astronaut
36 Be a Team Player
38 Fly to the Moon
40 Mission to Mars
42 Navigating in Space
44 Living in Space
46 Glossary
47 Further Information
48 Index

Traveling to Space

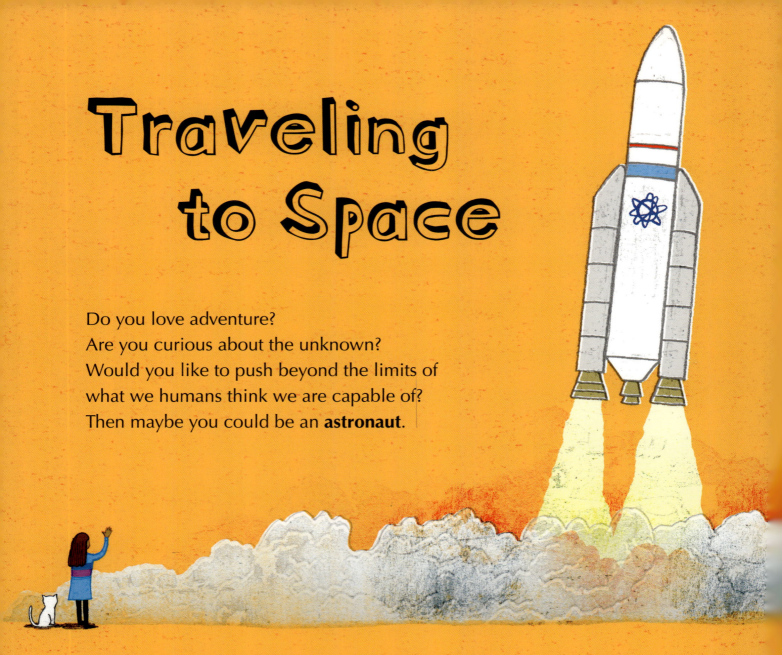

Do you love adventure?
Are you curious about the unknown?
Would you like to push beyond the limits of
what we humans think we are capable of?
Then maybe you could be an **astronaut**.

Why are we so fascinated by the idea of going into space? We are driven by an urge to explore the unknown, discover new things about our **solar system**, and make progress in science and technology.

The first thing to know about space is that it's a dangerous place for humans. There's no air, food, or water in space. In other words, there is nothing to support life. Yet these days, quite a number of people travel, work, and spend time beyond Earth's **atmosphere**. To do so, they must take equipment with them that supports life in their spacecraft.

The first human to venture into space was the Soviet **cosmonaut** Yuri Gagarin. He completed one orbit of Earth in 1961.

Later, from 1968 to 1972, American astronauts went on missions to the Moon.

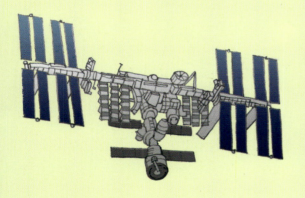

Today, we have a **space station** in orbit around Earth that always has a crew living on it. It's called the International Space Station (ISS). There are also plans to send missions with humans aboard back to the Moon and maybe even to Mars.

More astronauts will be needed for these future missions. To be an astronaut, you need to learn how to think like one. That means learning:

- how to make good decisions and stick to them
- how to **improvise** in tricky situations
- how to be self-sufficient.

Do you like the sound of that? If so, read this book and begin to train your brain to think like an astronaut.

Be Healthy and Fit

Space is tough on the human body. A rocket fires you up there at a tremendous speed, pushing you down into your seat at up to three times the force of gravity. Once you are in space, gravity is weaker than on Earth and you float around. Spending time in weightless conditions weakens the bones and muscles.

To cope with all this, you'll need to be healthy and fit. That means exercising regularly and eating a balanced diet rich in vitamins and minerals.

Astronauts have to concentrate on difficult tasks in space. Having a healthy body helps you to have a healthy mind, so you are better able to carry out these tasks. To boost your brain power, your diet should include foods such as green, leafy vegetables, fish, fruit, eggs, nuts, and berries.

To be an astronaut, you'll need to be fit. Regular exercise strengthens your muscles and bones. On the ISS there is a stationary bicycle, treadmill, and weightlifting machine. Astronauts use these for two hours each day.

Try some exercises to prepare you for the experience of being an astronaut.

Jump—Jumping helps to build strong bones.

Float—Lie on your stomach with legs and arms raised to strengthen your core.

Balance—Stand on one leg to develop core muscles and posture.

Stretch—Slowly fold your body over and try to touch your toes. The human body naturally stretches in space. The bones of the spine move apart slightly because they aren't being pushed down by gravity. This exercise will help your body get used to stretching.

At the end of your exercise session, relax for five minutes and focus on your breathing. This exercise will help to train your brain to deal with problems in a calm and efficient way.

Know How Things Work

Spacecraft are full of complicated machines. If one of these devices breaks down in space, you can't take it to a repair shop to get it fixed. To be an astronaut you need to know how the machines on your spacecraft work, so you can fix them if something goes wrong.

The ISS is the biggest spacecraft ever built and no one astronaut can understand how all of it works. So astronauts get training in particular systems, such as heating and cooling, or communications. Between them, the crew will have enough knowledge to fix most problems.

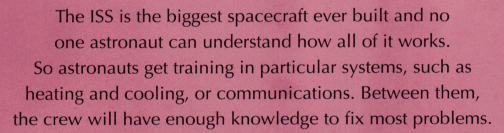

Before you receive your astronaut training, it helps to know the basics of how a spacecraft works. You will need an understanding of math, chemistry, and physics—the science of energy and matter—to understand the science of how rockets get into space.

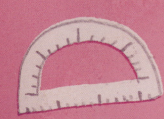

Rockets need plenty of **thrust** to overcome Earth's gravity. They have large tanks containing solid or liquid fuel. The fuel mixes with oxygen, creating a chemical reaction. The burning fuel produces exhaust gases that are forced out the back. This creates enough thrust to push the rocket forward.

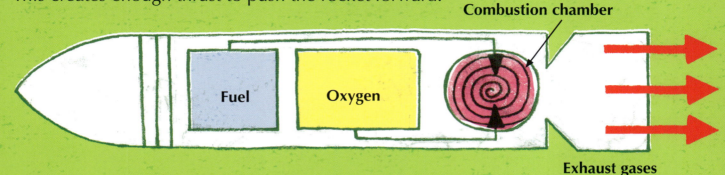

As a practical way of seeing how rockets work, why not make your own balloon rocket:

You will need: • balloon   • piece of string 10 to 13 feet (3 to 4 m) long   • straw   • sticky tape   • chair

1. Tie one end of the string to a door knob.
2. Pull the other end of the string through the straw.
3. Pull the string tight and tie the other end to a chair.
4. Blow up the balloon. Keep the hole end pinched between your fingers so the air can't escape.
5. Tape the balloon to the straw.
6. Let go and watch the rocket fly!

Neil Armstrong: First on the Moon

In 1969, American astronaut Neil Armstrong became the first human to set foot on the Moon. The idea that anyone could achieve such a feat would have seemed impossible at the time of his birth on August 5, 1930. At that time, the highest a rocket had flown was 88 feet (27 m). Spaceflight was just a dream.

Armstrong grew up in rural Ohio. His boyhood ambition was to become a pilot and **aeronautical** engineer, or someone who designs planes and jets. He took flying lessons when he was 15 and got his pilot's licence on his 16th birthday. Armstrong studied hard at school, especially math and science. He won a **scholarship** to university to study aeronautical engineering.

Later, Armstrong became a pilot in the U.S. Navy. During a mission in the **Korean War**, part of the wing of his aircraft was sliced off after a collision with a cable. He managed to fly his damaged plane back to friendly territory. This proved his coolness under pressure—a quality that would serve him well as an astronaut.

In 1962, Armstrong was accepted into the astronaut program run by the National Aeronautics and Space Administration (**NASA**). During the tough training, he was exposed to **acceleration**, vibration, and loud noise so he would know what to expect at launch. He trained in a giant swimming pool to learn how to move around in microgravity, or low gravity.

10

Armstrong's first mission was in NASA's Gemini human spaceflight program. He and his Gemini 8 crewmate performed the first ever **docking**, or joining of two spacecraft in orbit. At one point Gemini 8 started spinning out of control. Armstrong and his crewmate nearly blacked out. Armstrong saved the day by switching off the thrusters and switching on another system to stop the spin.

On July 16, 1969, Armstrong set off in Apollo 11 on his most famous mission: the first voyage to the surface of the Moon with a crew onboard. Four days later, he and his crewmate Buzz Aldrin descended to the Moon's surface in the **lunar module**, *Eagle*.

Armstrong needed all his training and experience for the landing. Despite computer problems and nearly running out of fuel, he piloted them safely to the surface. Several hours later, Armstrong stepped off the ladder of *Eagle*. He placed his foot on the Moon and said the immortal words: "That's one small step for [a] man, one giant leap for mankind."

Make Good Decisions

In space, things can sometimes go wrong. There might be a fire on board or your spacecraft could get hit by a piece of flying debris. You may have to make a quick decision to save the situation. Making good decisions and sticking to them is a skill you can learn. Why not give it a try?

Start small by making a simple decision and sticking to it for a month. For example, you could decide that every day for a month, you are going to do ten push-ups or learn five words in Japanese. See if you can stick to it.

As an astronaut, you often have to make a quick decision in a moment of crisis. It's important to keep a cool head. To help astronauts train for this, they are given difficult tasks to perform under time pressure.

Here are some tips on how to stay calm under pressure:

Breathe deeply and slowly—This helps your body relax.

Use your experience—Most problems are versions of problems you have encountered before, so let your training and experience guide you.

Focus on what's possible—Rather than worry about what is going wrong, think about the things you can do to help solve the problem.

Think about the next step—Instead of scaring yourself by dwelling on the worst possible outcome, ask yourself what is the next thing you should do.

To test how good you are at making decisions under pressure, try playing a game. It could be a quiz, chess, or a card game. Give each person a strict time limit for their turn.

Improvise to Survive

As an astronaut, sometimes you will face problems that you have not come across in your training and you will have to learn how to IMPROVISE! This means thinking creatively and using what is available to solve the problem.

During the Apollo 11 Moon landing in 1969, a switch broke off in the lunar module. Neil Armstrong and Buzz Aldrin were in danger of being stranded on the Moon. Buzz tried inserting a felt-tip pen in the opening where the switch should have been. Luckily, this worked!

We improvise all the time in our daily lives. Life rarely goes according to plan and we have to find ways to adapt. No bag to carry your books? Maybe you can wrap them in an old belt and carry them that way. Scratched phone screen? Dab a bit of toothpaste on it. When you wipe it off, the scratch will be much less visible.

Improvising is all about using your existing skills and knowledge and applying them to other problems. It means accepting the situation—however bad it may be—and finding ways of adapting. It means having an open, flexible mindset, not a closed, rigid one.
When asked if you can help, say "Yes, and...," not "Yes, but...."

Imagine you are a shipwreck survivor on a deserted island. Try improvising to survive. How will you find food, water, and shelter?

Change Your Perspective

Astronauts often speak of the wonder they feel when they first go up into space and how, when they see Earth looking so small, it changes their **perspective**. You can practice doing the same thing here on Earth simply by looking at things in a different way.

On December 24, 1968, Bill Anders, an astronaut on Apollo 8, took a famous photo of Earth rising over the Moon. People were able to look at Earth as a small, beautiful planet in a vast universe. It got people thinking about how important it is to protect our planet, and helped inspire the modern environmental movement.

To think like an astronaut, you must never lose your sense of wonder. Here are some ways of reminding yourself how incredible our world and universe are:

Seek out amazing things—Visit a museum, art gallery, or planetarium. Look at photos from the ISS to see Earth as astronauts do.

Imagine you're somebody else—As you walk through your neighborhood, try seeing it through the eyes of a visitor. Reintroduce yourself to your familiar surroundings so they seem fresh again.

Slow down—Take the time to observe the world around you. Notice the dance of dragonflies, the singing of birds, and the scent of flowers.

These techniques will allow you to step out of your everyday life for a while and help you see things differently.

Yi So-yeon: First South Korean in Space

Yi So-yeon was born on June 2, 1978, and grew up in Gwangju, South Korea. She studied hard at school and went on to earn a master's degree in mechanical engineering at the Korea Advanced Institute of Science and Technology. While working for her **doctorate** in biological science, Yi applied to become an astronaut through the Korean Astronaut Program. She was selected as one of two finalists out of 36,000 applicants!

On April 8, 2008, Yi became South Korea's first astronaut when she launched into space aboard a Soyuz TMA-12 rocket. Her spacecraft docked with the ISS. There she spent nearly 11 days carrying out 18 scientific experiments and medical tests. Yi measured the effects of microgravity on fruit flies, plant seeds, and her own heart, eyes, and face shape. She observed the movement of dust storms from China to Korea.

During her stay on the space station, Yi never tired of observing Earth. She would wake up in the middle of the night and float over to her cabin's window for another look. Yi believes our planet is a gift and we have a duty to preserve it.

Something went wrong on the return flight to Earth, and Yi So-yeon and her fellow astronauts nearly died. Their Soyuz spacecraft malfunctioned as they re-entered Earth's atmosphere. The capsule briefly turned upside down, exposing the wrong side to the fierce temperatures caused by the **friction** of re-entry. If it had continued like this for a few seconds longer, the astronauts might have been killed. During their unusually steep descent to Earth, they experienced up to 10 times the normal amount of gravity. The astronauts had a rough landing in Kazakhstan, 260 miles (418 km) from their target. But they survived with few injuries.

Throughout the crisis, Yi continued to think like an astronaut, remaining calm and doing her job. "I could feel the shock and vibration," she said, "but there was nothing I could do except [focus] on my own job and protocol."

Her adventure in space put life into perspective for Yi. "It is easy to complain about a low signal on your phone, or traffic, crowds, or noise. But all those things exist because you live on the most comfortable planet in space. Be glad you have a phone."

Floating Free

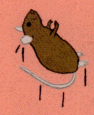

We don't usually think about gravity. But many of our everyday activities, such as moving around, washing, eating, sleeping, and using the toilet, have to be done quite differently in the microgravity of a space station.

To be an astronaut, you have to train your brain to work in a completely different way. "Up" and "down" mean very little in space. To move around, you use your hands as much as your legs. Anything not tied down will float, so you need to train your brain to be very organized if you don't want to lose things.

You will need to get used to things not having as much flavor because you can't taste and smell as well in microgravity. Cakes and cookies are impossible to eat on the ISS because the crumbs float everywhere! Salt and pepper can be used, but only in liquid form.

In microgravity, water forms into a ball and floats, so you can't take a bath or shower. Instead, you squeeze a ball of soapy water out of a packet, catch it in your hands and wash yourself with it. Using the toilet is complicated. It involves using suction to pull waste into tubes and bags. You will need to get used to new ways of doing these everyday things.

Try to imagine how you would go about your daily activities if everything, including you, floated. What would school be like? What kind of sports and games would you play? How would you sleep?

Prepare to Be Lonely

Space missions can be long. Astronauts often spend months at a time on space stations with just a few crewmates for company. In the future, space missions are likely to get longer as astronauts travel to a base on the Moon, or on a mission to Mars.

To think like an astronaut, you need to be self-reliant and not too dependent on the company of friends and family. There are ways of training yourself to be self-reliant:

Create a daily routine of work, exercise, meals, and relaxation to give your day structure.

Enjoy time with your friends and family, but also develop hobbies you can do by yourself, such as reading, photography, or playing a musical instrument. Try keeping a journal, and make it part of your end-of-day routine to write about your thoughts, feelings, and activities.

Astronauts have to work on their social skills, too. They will chat, play games, share stories from home, and try to stay in touch with Earth. Having a normal conversation with anyone on Earth will be impossible from Mars. Communication signals take between 3 and 22 minutes to travel between the two planets. Astronauts will still be able to keep up with news from Earth, just not instantaneously.

Why not get into the habit of writing a journal now? Being able to summarize your day in a few paragraphs is a useful skill for any budding astronaut. Future historians will read astronaut journals to learn about what life was like for the early settlers on other planets. You never know, yours might be one they will study.

Communicate

As an astronaut you will need good communication skills. They might even save your life! If there's a problem or emergency on board your spacecraft, you'll need to be able to explain precisely what's wrong to the team back on Earth and understand their advice.

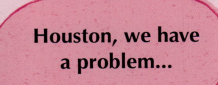

Houston, we have a problem...

Astronauts are expected to be in regular communication with Mission Control on Earth. They also need to speak to the media and the public, telling them about life in space.

To be an astronaut, you need to be able to speak confidently, with clear pronunciation, so you can be understood even on a crackly radio. You also need to speak precisely and keep to the point. This is especially useful on a spacewalk (see pages 28–29), when your time and air supply is limited.

Communication is just as much about listening as speaking. Astronauts need to listen carefully to advice and instructions. If anything is unclear, they should ask the speaker to repeat it. In space, where a misunderstanding could spell disaster, it's always worth double checking what someone means.

Could you repeat that, please?

Today, many countries are sending people into space, so communication isn't confined to one language. As an astronaut, learning another language such as Russian, Chinese, or Japanese could be a useful or vital skill.

To test your speaking and listening skills, try playing the game Telephone.

You will need five or more players. Form yourselves into a line. The person at one end whispers a message to the person next to them, who whispers it to the next person, and so on. When the final person in the line hears the message, they say what they think the message was. Did the message change along the way?

Mae Jemison: Astronaut, Doctor, and Engineer

Mae Carol Jemison, the first Black woman to go into space, was born on October 17, 1956, in Alabama, and grew up in Chicago. From an early age, she loved to dance, but also knew that she wanted to study science. As a teenager, Jemison watched the Apollo space missions on TV and was upset that there were no female astronauts. She decided she wanted to go to space one day.

At school, Jemison spent a lot of her time in the library, reading about all aspects of science—especially astronomy. She also studied languages, becoming fluent in Russian, Japanese, and Swahili.

After earning a degree in chemical engineering from Stanford University, Jemison attended Cornell Medical School where, in 1981, she earned a doctorate in medicine. For the next few years, she practiced medicine in Los Angeles, California. She also served with the **Peace Corps** in Liberia and Sierra Leone, Africa.

In 1987, Jemison applied to NASA to be an astronaut. She was selected as one of 15 from more than 2,000 applicants. Jemison was awarded the title Science Mission Specialist and was responsible for conducting scientific experiments on board the **space shuttle**.

Jemison's previous experiences helped her during her astronaut training. One test that the instructors asked her to do was to pluck and gut a dead bird. "For some reason they decided they wanted to pick on me [and] I'm probably the worst person to pick on," she said. "I'm a doctor. You can't gross me out."

On September 12, 1992, Jemison and six other astronauts flew into space aboard the space shuttle *Endeavour*. They made 127 orbits around Earth, returning on September 20, 1992. While aboard, Jemison carried out a number of experiments, studying the effects of weightlessness and motion sickness on both herself and other crew members. In another experiment, she investigated how frog eggs and tadpoles developed in microgravity.

Today, Jemison leads the 100 Year Starship Project, which aims to encourage the research and technology needed to send humans to other star systems within 100 years.

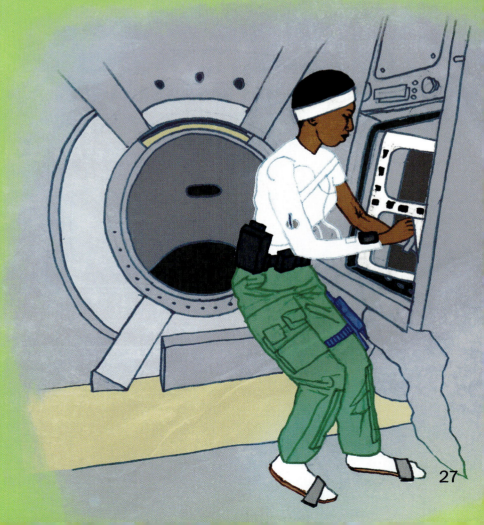

Train for a Spacewalk

Sometimes astronauts must go on spacewalks. These are trips outside the spacecraft wearing a spacesuit in order to carry out repairs or conduct science experiments. Spacewalks take a lot of mental and physical training.

A successful spacewalk requires PLANNING. With limited oxygen supplies, astronauts will need to work efficiently, so each stage needs to be measured in advance. The astronaut meets with their team to discuss the spacewalk. They rank jobs in order of importance, so they know what to do first. They work out an efficient route for the spacewalk.

You can practice this by planning a route for a walk that takes you to three different places in the shortest amount of time.

Spacewalkers need to be CAREFUL and PATIENT. After getting into their spacesuits, astronauts perform a "leak check" to ensure they are fully protected against the **vacuum** of space. They spend several hours breathing pure oxygen, ridding their bodies of nitrogen so they don't suffer a painful condition known as "the bends." They must be careful. If you breathe pure oxygen for more than 16 hours, it can cause permanent lung damage.

Once outside their spacecraft, astronauts need to be AGILE. Carrying things, screwing in a bolt, or plugging in an electrical cord may be simple tasks on Earth, but doing this in microgravity while wearing big spacesuit gloves takes practice.
How many activities can you do while wearing thick gloves?

Under the supervision of an adult, practice spacewalking maneuvers, or drills, the next time you go swimming. Try pushing a beachball from one side of the pool to the other or picking up a coin from the bottom.

Be Curious and Observant

The International Space Station (ISS) is an orbiting laboratory. Astronauts spend a lot of their day conducting scientific experiments. To be an astronaut, you will need to think like a scientist. That means asking questions, testing theories, and recording the results.

Astronauts study the behavior of materials, plants, and animals in microgravity. They examine the effects of microgravity on human beings. This helps prepare them for future space missions. They observe Earth with powerful sensors, collecting information about climate change and recording natural disasters in real time.

You can train your brain to be an astronaut-scientist by being curious, observant, and open-minded. In microgravity, you should always expect the unexpected. For example, in space, flames tend to be shaped like a sphere, not the tear-drop shape we see on Earth.

Ask yourself questions, then come up with a **hypothesis** to test it. For instance, what might be the problem with growing food plants in microgravity? What could you do to ensure water gets to the plant's roots?

Try this space-themed science experiment.

Aim: to see how the size of a **meteorite** is related to the size of the crater it makes on impact

You will need:
- large cardboard box   • bag of flour   • ruler
- 3 spherical objects of different sizes, e.g. golf ball, tennis ball, grapefruit

Instructions:
1. Pour the flour into the box so it is spread evenly.
2. Drop each object into the box from the same height to create three craters.
3. Measure the diameter of each crater and record the results in a notebook.

Conclusion:
Do you notice any pattern between the size of the "meteorite" and the size of the crater it makes?

31

Develop Your Piloting Skills

The job of a pilot astronaut is to control and operate spacecraft, dock with the ISS, land on surfaces, and return the spacecraft safely to Earth. All of this takes a lot of training.

Many astronauts begin their careers as military or test pilots. This gives them important skills that prepare them for flying in space.

You can start this process by training your brain in a few basic skills.

One important skill is spatial awareness. This means the ability to understand and interact with the environment around you, so you can avoid crashing into things. Pilots need this to stay aware of where they and their spacecraft are in relation to Earth or another spacecraft while in flight.

You can develop your spatial awareness by running obstacle courses, constructing things with building blocks, and doing jigsaw puzzles.

Another important skill for pilot astronauts is coordination. This is the ability to use different parts of your body together, smoothly and efficiently. Try these exercises to improve your coordination:

- **For hand-eye coordination:** Practice throwing and catching a ball. Or play tennis, table tennis, baseball, or football.
- **For right-left coordination:** Cycle, swim, climb up a ladder (supervised by an adult).
- **For hand skills:** Skip some flat stones on water, or roll dough or modeling clay with both hands, play the piano, or learn to type.
- **For balance:** Stand on one leg, walk backward, or hop on one leg.

As a pilot astronaut, you will often have to react quickly in high-pressure situations. That's why you need good spatial awareness and coordination skills.

33

Chris Hadfield: The Singing Astronaut

Chris Hadfield was born on August 29, 1959, in Sarnia, Ontario, Canada. He was an adventurous boy who by his teens was an expert skier. Having watched the Apollo 11 Moon landing on TV, he dreamed of becoming an astronaut. But Canada had no astronaut program, so Hadfield decided to fly planes instead.

In 1978, Hadfield joined the Canadian Armed Forces and went to military college. In the 1980s, he flew fighter and bomber aircraft for the Canadian and U.S. militaries. By the early 1990s, he had flown more than 70 kinds of planes.

When Canada launched its own astronaut program, Hadfield applied. He was selected in June 1992, joining the team at the NASA Space Center in Houston. He did many jobs for NASA, including communicating with astronauts in space shuttles and on the ISS.

Hadfield also made three trips to space. In 1995, he flew on the space shuttle *Atlantis* and docked with the Russian space station Mir. In 2001, he flew on the space shuttle *Endeavour*, delivering a new Canadian-built robotic arm to the ISS. During this 11-day mission he became the first Canadian to walk in space.

Hadfield's greatest space adventure began in December 2012, when he blasted off in a Soyuz rocket for a five-month stay aboard the ISS. He became a global celebrity during this mission with his regular tweets about life in space. As an accomplished singer and guitarist, he spent his free time playing music. Hadfield's version of *Space Oddity* by David Bowie was recorded on the space station and received millions of views.

Since retiring from the Canadian Space Agency, Hadfield has spent his time writing books, giving talks, and making TV shows about his life as an astronaut and what it has taught him. He compares life's journey to that of a spacecraft moving through space. He says that you can't always control what happens to you, but you should do everything in your power to stay on your chosen path. Losing your way, says Hadfield, is much worse than not reaching your destination.

Be a Team Player

Astronauts don't make it to space on their own. They need to work closely with their fellow crew members and with Mission Control. Everyone needs to share the same goals and know their role and position within the team.

Being part of a team sometimes means leading, sometimes following. Each astronaut has their own particular set of skills. If you're new to a situation, it's usually better to listen to those with more experience. But if you know what to do, it's okay to take charge. The best way to lead is to set an example for others to follow and build agreement for a particular course of action. Don't bully people into following you.

On long space missions, tensions can build within a team, just as they can among families and friends on Earth. A good team player will always try to lighten the mood with **empathy** and humor. They will also look for practical ways to resolve conflicts.

Here's a team-building activity you can try with friends.

You are on a mission to Mars. Due to a mechanical error you were forced to land 50 miles (80 km) from base camp. You and your crew can only carry seven objects from your spacecraft to base, so you must choose which ones are most important. First, everyone should fill out this list:

Items	My ranking	Team ranking
portable storm shelter		
box of matches		
food supplies		
nylon rope		
oxygen tanks		
star map		
magnetic compass		
water		
signal flares		
first aid kit		
solar-powered radio		
portable heating unit		

Check out pages 40-41 for some information about Mars. Next, each team member should allocate a number to each item between 1 and 12, with number 1 for the highest-ranking item. Then get together with the other team members to share thoughts and ideas and come up with an agreed team ranking.

FLY TO THE MOON

Space agencies are planning to send new missions with crews aboard to the Moon and eventually build a base there. As a budding astronaut, you should learn all you can about the Moon, Earth's only natural satellite, and think about the skills and experience you will need to survive there.

To set up a base camp on the Moon, you will need: air, water, food, energy, and shelter.

Air: Lunar soil is 42 percent oxygen. Using a simple process involving heat and electricity, you can harvest the oxygen. You will need some chemistry skills for this.

Water: There's ice on the Moon, mainly at the poles. You'll need some mapping and navigation skills to find the ice and mining expertise to drill it out. With a knowledge of chemistry, you could split water into its elements of oxygen and hydrogen, both of which can be used for fuel.

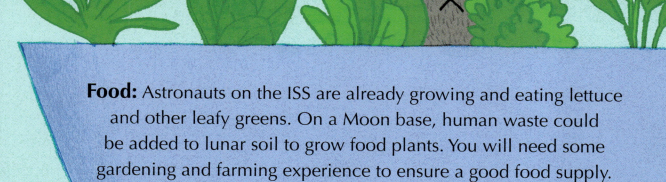

Food: Astronauts on the ISS are already growing and eating lettuce and other leafy greens. On a Moon base, human waste could be added to lunar soil to grow food plants. You will need some gardening and farming experience to ensure a good food supply.

Energy: Lunar soil contains all the materials to build solar panels. If placed on the Moon's poles, these could receive permanent sunlight and provide limitless power. Engineering skills would be crucial here.

Shelter: Settlers would need protection from **radiation** and meteorites. They could live in inflatable shelters at first. Later, they could print bricks from lunar soil using a 3-D printer. They could live under cliffs, in caves, or underground in lava tubes formed by ancient volcanoes. You will need to be good at building things to set up Moon shelters.

Mission to Mars

One day we hope to send humans to Mars. As an astronaut going on such a mission, you would have to be well-trained and prepared for anything. Mars is a long way from Earth and many things could go wrong.

As a Mars astronaut, you would need mental strength because the mission will take many months, or even years. You would need to deal with loneliness. You would train in a special module in a remote place, such as a desert or the Arctic, where you can get used to living an isolated life with your fellow crew members.

To be a Mars astronaut, you would need to be practical and resourceful. If an important machine breaks, you and your crew will have to repair it since it could be months before a replacement arrives from Earth.

You would also need to be resilient, which is the ability to adjust and recover well from setbacks. Mars is a freezing desert planet, colder than Antarctica. It has no air and very low gravity. Frequent dust storms cover its entire surface for weeks, blocking out sunlight. You would be confined to your artificial habitat, except for trips outside in your spacesuit or in a vehicle to repair a solar panel or mine resources for fuel, water, and oxygen.

Each crew member would have different skills and experience. The mission would need medical experts, engineers, and technicians, as well as experts on Martian rocks and microscopic alien life forms.

Which kind of expert would you like to be?

NAVIGATING IN SPACE

One day, we might send astronauts on missions into deep space, or the farthest reaches of the solar system and beyond. How would you find your way to other planets? It would take very different navigation skills from those you use to find your way around Earth.

On Earth you can use reference points, such as the Sun and stars, to determine your position and direction. In space there are no fixed reference points because everything is moving. Your spacecraft, along with the planet or moon you are heading for, may be traveling at thousands of miles per hour.

Only a computer is capable of making the hundreds of complex calculations necessary to determine your location at any particular moment. You will need excellent IT skills since you will be using your computer a lot.

As you move through space, your craft will always be pulled by the gravity of some large body. It could be Earth, another planet, a moon, or a star. In other words, you'll always be in orbit around something. Before you set off, you must figure out your craft's "trajectory." This is your path through these various orbits that will take you to your destination. For this, you'll need a good understanding of the physics of forces and motion.

After launch, your on-board computer will regularly report your spacecraft's position to navigators back on Earth. If you go off course, the navigators will tell you to adjust your position using rocket boosters.

You will hurtle through space at incredible speeds. Decisions to change course will need to be made quickly, so you will need to think fast and react quickly.

To find your way in space, you'll need computer skills, a knowledge of physics, and a quick mind.

Living in Space

In the distant future, we might build enormous space stations in orbit around Earth where people could live permanently. It'll take some imagination to think about what it might be like to live off-world. What do you think the main challenges would be?

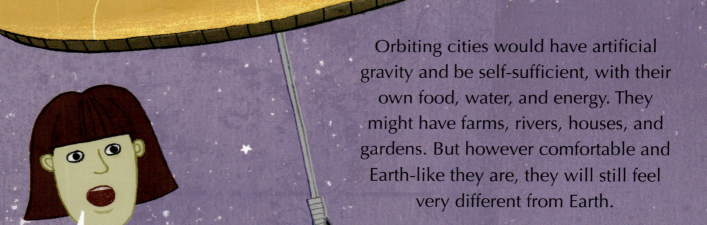

Orbiting cities would have artificial gravity and be self-sufficient, with their own food, water, and energy. They might have farms, rivers, houses, and gardens. But however comfortable and Earth-like they are, they will still feel very different from Earth.

As an off-worlder, you would spend your life in an enclosed space with no sense of ever being "outside." Orbiting Earth 16 times every 24 hours, you would have a different sense of time, with days and nights flashing by every 90 minutes. You would have an artificially controlled climate, and the weather would always be temperate.

Your space community would soon develop its own culture, fashion, architecture, art, and music. You would have your own words for things. Eventually, you might even form your own language. Can you think of any words you might need as an off-worlder? What words might be lost from your Earth language?

Earth will always remain your "mother planet," but eventually Earthlings would start to seem quite different from you. This division would be even more apparent for your children who would be born and raised in space.

Imagine your space community wants to become an independent country. Design a flag for it and create a set of laws. If you feel inspired, why not write the words to a national anthem?

45

Glossary

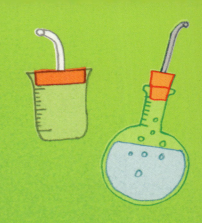

acceleration Increasing speed

aeronautical Relating to the science of building or flying aircraft

astronaut A person trained for space flight

atmosphere The gases surrounding a planet

cosmonaut A Russian astronaut

docking To join to vehicles, or stations, in space

doctorate The highest degree awarded by a university

empathy The ability to understand and share feelings

friction The resistance that one surface encounters when moving over another

hypothesis A proposed explanation used as a starting point of scientific investigation

improvise To make or perform something without preparation or from whatever is available

Korean War A war between North and South Korea (1950–53), aided by their allies

lunar module A small craft used for traveling between the Moon's surface and an orbiting spacecraft

meteorite A particle of matter found in space, known as a space rock, that has fallen to Earth

NASA National Aeronautics and Space Administration—the U.S. space agency

Peace Corps A U.S. government volunteer program that provides aid to other countries

perspective A way of looking at something

radiation The emission of energy as waves or as tiny particles

scholarship A grant or payment made to support a student's education, awarded because of academic achievement

solar system The planets, moons, asteroids, and other bodies in orbit around the Sun

space shuttle A spacecraft that was launched by a rocket and could land like an aircraft

space station An orbiting, crewed station in space

thrust The force created by a jet or rocket engine that pushes the craft forward

vacuum Something that contains no air or any kind of matter

Further Information

Books

Astronomers in Action. Anne Rooney. Crabtree Publishing, 2018.
Discover the fascinating world of working scientists and see how they investigate problems and work together on solutions. Mini-bios introduce readers to leading lights in the field of astronomy.

Top Secret Science in Space. Honor Head. Crabtree Publishing, 2019.
Investigate closely guarded secrets and scientific developments that pushed space exploration in the past and helped our knowledge of space expand.

Watch This Space (series). Various authors. Crabtree Publishing, 2015.
This fascinating series on astronomy, space exploration, and secrets of the universe features brilliant images and diagrams that help readers understand how vast space is and how humans are just beginning to understand many aspects of how it works and how space exploration will change in the future.

Our Future in Space (series). Various Authors. Crabtree Publishing, 2018.
These books on space colonization, exploration, tourism, and workers peer into the future of space exploration and how humans could live and thrive in space and on other planets.

Websites

www.nasa.gov/kidsclub/index.html
The website of NASA Kids' Club is a huge and fascinating resource. It includes information about the history of NASA and regular updates on current missions. There are loads of photos, videos, and blogs. You can even tune into the NASA TV channel.

https://airandspace.si.edu
The Smithsonian's Air and Space Museum has information on exhibits and collections as well as clickable videos, podcasts, and read-a-loud books and stories on planets, space, astronomy, and space exploration.

www.nationalgeographic.com/science/space/our-solar-system/
This website from National Geographic tells you all you need to know about our solar system. It describes the planets and the many other objects that travel around the Sun. The informative text is supplemented by stunning videos and slide shows.

www.stardate.org
Learn all about stargazing and what can be seen in the sky from where you live. This website has lesson plans and activities for teachers and learning groups, an astroguide image section and an astroglossary of words and meanings.

Index

Aldrin, Buzz 11, 14
Anders, Bill 16
Apollo 11 11, 14, 34
Armstrong, Neil 10–11, 14
atmosphere 4, 19

bases on Moon and Mars 22, 37, 38, 39
bathing 21

communication 23, 24–25, 34
computers 42, 43
coordination 33

decision-making 5, 12, 13
docking 11, 18, 32, 34

Earth 4, 5, 6, 9, 16, 17, 18, 19, 23, 24, 30, 32, 36, 40, 42, 43, 44
energy 38, 39, 44
exercise 6, 7, 22

fitness 6, 7
food 4, 6, 15, 21, 22, 31, 37, 38, 39, 44
fuel 9, 11, 38, 41

Gagarin, Yuri 4
gravity 6, 9, 19, 20, 41, 43, 44

Hadfield, Chris 34–35
health 6, 22

improvisation 5, 14–15
International Space Station (ISS) 5, 7, 8, 17, 18, 30, 32, 34, 35, 39

Jemison, Mae 26–27

lunar module 11

Mars 5, 22, 23, 37, 40
microgravity 10, 18, 20–21, 27, 30, 31
Mission Control 24, 34, 36
Moon 4, 5, 10, 11, 14, 16, 22, 38–39

NASA 10, 27, 34
navigation 38, 42–43

orbiting 4, 5, 43, 44
oxygen 9, 28, 29, 37, 38, 41

pilot astronauts 32–33

rockets 8, 9, 10, 18, 35

scientific experiments 18, 27, 28, 30
self-sufficiency 5, 22–23, 40, 44
shelter 15, 37, 38, 39
solar system 5, 42
spacecraft 4, 11, 12, 24, 28, 32, 37, 42, 43
space shuttles 27, 34
space stations 5, 20, 22, 34, 44
spacesuits 28, 41
spacewalks 24, 28–29, 34
spatial awareness 32, 33

teamwork 36–37
training 8, 10, 12, 13, 27, 28, 32, 40

water 4, 15, 21, 31, 37, 38, 41, 44

Yi So-yeon 18–19